EXPLORING THE ELEMENTS

Silver

Henrietta Toth

Enslow Publishing
101 W. 23rd Street
Suite 240
New York, NY 10011
USA

enslow.com

Published in 2019 by Enslow Publishing, LLC.
101 W. 23rd Street, Suite 240, New York, NY 10011

Library of Congress Cataloging-in-Publication Data

Names: Toth, Henrietta, author.
Title: Silver / Henrietta Toth.
Description: New York : Enslow Publishing, [2019] | Series: Exploring the elements | Audience: Grades 5-7 | Includes bibliographical references and index.
Identifiers: LCCN 2017052658| ISBN 9780766099265 (library bound) | ISBN 9780766099272 (pbk.)
Subjects: LCSH: Silver—Juvenile literature. | Chemical elements—Juvenile literature. | Precious metals—Juvenile literature.
Classification: LCC TN761.6 .T68 2018 | DDC 546/.654—dc23
LC record available at https://lccn.loc.gov/2017052658

Printed in the United States of America

Portions of this book appeared in *Silver* by Brian Belval, Jun Lim.

To Our Readers: We have done our best to make sure all website addresses in this book were active and appropriate when we went to press. However, the author and the publisher have no control over and assume no liability for the material available on those websites or on any websites they may link to. Any comments or suggestions can be sent by email to customerservice@enslow.com.

Photo Credits: Cover, p. 1 TK-1980/Shutterstock.com; p. 8 VladKK/Shutterstock.com; p. 10 Everett Historical/Shutterstock.com; p. 12 ColinCramm/Shutterstock.com; p. 16 Designua/Shutterstock.com; p. 17 88studio/Shutterstock.com; p. 19 tanrun1970/Shutterstock.com; p. 22 bambambu/Shutterstock.com; p. 24 George Ostertag/Alamy Stock Photo; p. 26 Greenshoots Communications/Alamy Stock Photo; p. 29 De Agostini/G. Cigolini/De Agostini Picture Library; p. 31 Andrew Lambert Photography/Science Source; p. 34 Perry Correll/Shutterstock.com; p. 37 aopsan/Shutterstock.com; p. 39 Hnatyk/Shutterstock.com; p. 41 Sofiart/Shutterstock.com.

Contents

Introduction

//

Taking a digital photograph today is as commonplace and as easy as lifting a cell phone, pointing it, and clicking. It was not that easy in the early days of photography.

The element and metal silver played a vital role in the development of photography. In the 1830s, silver enabled photographs to capture a scene or person as the human eye saw it instead of how the painter interpreted it. Two Frenchmen, Nicéphore Niépce (1765–1833) and Louis Daguerre (1789–1851), took the first photographs by combining silver and iodine. The silver iodide was thinly spread onto a sheet of metal, which was then placed into a camera box and exposed to light. The result was a black-and-white photograph.

Today, silver is a part of everyday life: cell phones used for communicating and taking pictures contain silver; batteries, mirrors, and DVDs contain silver; solar panels for homes and businesses are manufactured with silver, with the metal used in a paste that catches the sun's rays and converts them into energy. Since the fourteenth century, artists have used silver in making stained glass. The metal is applied to the back of the glass before the glass is heated in a kiln. The silver reacts with the glass and the stain to create various shades of yellow and orange.

Silver also plays a part in scientific and medical communities. The chemical compound silver iodide is used in cloud seeding to modify the weather, specifically in areas affected by drought. Silver iodide is sprayed into clouds from an airplane. The silver iodide causes water droplets to form into ice crystals, which then fall from the cloud. As the ice crystals fall, they melt and turn into rain. Silver has long been used in medicine. Before the discovery of antibiotics, wounds were sometimes wrapped with silver foil to help them heal. Silver iodide is also applied as an antiseptic because of its antibiotic properties and low toxicity.

Silver is one of the rare metals on Earth, yet it has been used for thousands of years. Archaeologists have found silver objects in Greece and modern-day Turkey that date to before 4000 BCE. Ancient civilizations from Egypt to Europe used silver to make jewelry and coins. Silver's shiny, gray-white appearance, unique among metals, only increased its value.

Silver is also a chemical element. Its symbol is Ag on the periodic table, which stands for the Greek word *argentum*. Silver is a soft metal, but can be combined with other metals to harden it. This is how the alloy, or mixture, sterling silver is made.

The extraordinary properties of silver have made it a very useful and much relied upon metal throughout time. New ways of using silver are always emerging. Technological advances determine how silver continues to be included in everything from electronics to medicine.

1

A Valuable Element

Silver is one of more than one hundred elements that make up the known universe. Silver is not easy to find—in fact, it is only the sixty-sixth most abundant element on Earth. Because it is rare and can be shaped into jewelry and coins, silver has been valued by different civilizations for thousands of years. In ancient Egypt and medieval Europe, silver was more valuable than gold. However, in today's international market, gold is about seventy times more expensive than silver.

Parts of a Silver Atom

Silver, like all matter, is made of tiny particles called atoms. Atoms are made of even smaller particles: electrons, protons, and neutrons. At

A bullion bar of silver is typically used for trade on a market. It is named after French Minister of Finance Claude de Bullion, who served under Louis XIII in the 1600s.

the center of every atom is the nucleus. The nucleus consists of protons and neutrons packed together. Protons have a positive charge while neutrons have no charge. The nucleus is the solid core of the atom. A silver atom always has forty-seven protons in its nucleus. This is what makes an element different from all the other elements: they have different numbers of protons. For example, the hydrogen atom has one proton in its nucleus, while the gold atom has seventy-nine.

Electrons are negatively charged and are attracted to the positively charged protons. The attraction is similar to the way opposite poles of a magnet attract each other. Electrons are small and light. They weigh about two thousand times less than a proton or neutron. The electrons move around outside the nucleus in paths known as shells. Each atom can have multiple shells to hold the electrons; the silver atom has five shells of electrons. Two electrons are found in the first shell, eight in the second, eighteen in the third shell, eighteen in the fourth shell, and one in the fifth.

In all the elements, the electrons in the outer shell are known as the valence electrons. These electrons are interesting to chemists because they allow atoms to interact with other atoms. This process is known as chemical bonding.

In each atom, the number of electrons is always equal to the number of protons. This balances out the positive and negative charges. If an atom gains or loses an electron, it is known as an ion. An atom that has lost one or more electrons has a positive charge and is called a cation. An atom that has gained one or more electrons has a negative charge and is called an anion.

Silver's Isotopes

Atoms always have an equal number of protons and electrons (forty-seven in a silver atom), but the number of neutrons does not always match. Often, there are more neutrons than either protons or electrons.

The number of neutrons in an atom of an element can vary slightly. These atoms are known as isotopes. Silver has two isotopes: an

The Daguerreotype

Louis Daguerre invented a photographic process called the daguerreotype. Before the daguerreotype, it took about eight hours to capture a photographic image. For about fifteen years, Daguerre and his partner, Nicéphore Niépce, worked on a way to speed up the process. In 1839, Daguerre announced the invention of the daguerreotype, a process that used an iodized silver plate and required only thirty minutes of exposure time. Daguerreotypes had to be handled carefully because they were delicate and could be easily damaged when touched or exposed to moisture.

Mary Todd Lincoln, wife of President Abraham Lincoln, is shown in a daguerreotype photograph.

atom with sixty neutrons and an atom with sixty-two neutrons. Scientists have calculated that 52 percent of all silver atoms have sixty neutrons, while the other 48 percent have sixty-two neutrons.

Silver is not the only element that has isotopes. For example, carbon has a famous isotope known as carbon-14. This isotope of carbon has eight neutrons and is radioactive. It breaks down over thousands of years. By comparing the amount of carbon-14 in a sample to the amount of carbon-12 isotope (carbon atoms with six neutrons), scientists can determine the age of the sample. This method is known as carbon dating.

Organizing the Elements

An easier way to understand the elements is to take a look at the periodic table. In the table, the elements are organized into rows and columns. The rows are known as periods and the columns are known as groups. Each period and each group has a number. The periods are numbered 1 to 7, from top to bottom. The groups are numbered in one of two ways, depending on the version of the periodic table.

In the first system, the groups are numbered 1 to 18, from left to right. The second numbering system uses Roman numerals (I through VIII) followed by a letter (A or B), except for the noble gases at the far right, which are in group O. In this numbering system, the elements in the groups marked with an A are known as the representative elements. In the representative elements, the Roman numeral in the group equals the number of electrons in the outer shell of an element in that group. For example, elements in group VA have five electrons in their outer shell. Elements marked with a B are known as the transition metals. However, unlike the representative elements, the number before B in each of these groups does not always equal the number of outer-shell electrons. Like the transition

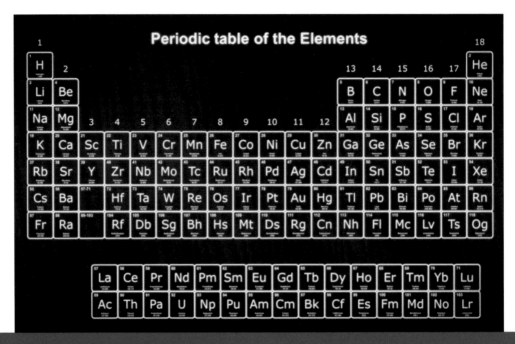

The periodic table presents the elements in neat groups and periods for easy identification.

metals, the noble gas elements also have varying numbers of electrons in their outer shells.

Below the main table is a smaller table consisting of two rows and fourteen columns. This block is part of the main table but has been cut out so the table is not too wide to fit across two pages. The first row of the smaller table should go in between barium and hafnium on the main table. These elements are known as the lanthanides. The second row of the smaller table goes between radium and rutherfordium. These elements are known as the actinides.

Each element occupies one square of the table. In group 11 (IB), row 5, is silver. The letter or letters that represent an element are known as its chemical symbol. Silver's chemical symbol is Ag, which is short for *argentum,* silver's name in Latin. A few of the other elements also have Latin abbreviations, such as gold (Au for *aurum)* and iron (Fe for *ferrum).*

There are two numbers In each square of the periodic table. The smaller number on the top left is called the atomic number. It is equal to the number of protons in an atom of the element. The atomic number increases from left to right going down the table. The larger number on the top right of each square is the atomic weight. The atomic weight is the sum of the number of protons and the average number of neutrons in an atom of the element.

The atomic weight and atomic number can be used to estimate the number of neutrons in an atom of a specific element. This calculation is not exact, but it offers a good estimate of the number of neutrons in an atom of a specific element:

atomic weight – atomic number = average number of neutrons

In the case of silver:

107.868 – 47 = 60.868 neutrons

According to this formula, an atom of silver has 60.868 neutrons. However, an atom can only consist of whole numbers of neutrons, not fractions. Therefore, the average number of neutrons in a silver atom is sixty-one. In reality, as noted earlier, an atom of silver has either sixty or sixty-two neutrons. This formula can only approximate the number of neutrons.

The Periodic Table Setup

The periodic table contains much useful information. The numbers on the table help to calculate the exact number of protons and electrons in an atom of an element, and also the approximate number of neutrons.

A lot can be learned about an element simply from its location on the periodic table. This is because the elements in a group often share chemical properties. A chemical property refers to how the element reacts with other substances. For example, all the elements in column IA react with water, releasing bubbles of hydrogen gas.

Silver is part of a large group spanning the middle of the table, known as the transition metals. The elements of group IB are called "coinage metals" because they have been used in coins and are not very reactive (they do not corrode as iron does). The transition metals also have similar traits, including the ability to conduct heat and electricity, and the capability to be pounded into sheets and to be stretched into wires.

2

Silver's Physical and Chemical Properties

//

hemists identify elements by their physical and chemical properties. Chemical properties refers to how elements react with other elements or substances. These reactions result in an element being changed into something else. Physical properties, on the other hand, can be observed without reacting or changing an element into other substances. These properties include color, hardness, melting point, and density.

STATE OF MATTER

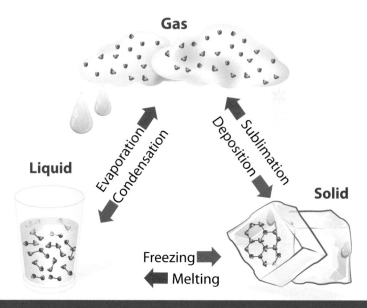

Every kind of matter exists in three states: solid, liquid, or gas. Water can be the liquid you drink, the ice you slip on, or the steam that powers a train.

Silver's Physical States

Matter exists in three phases: solid, liquid, and gas. Think about water. Water in its liquid phase is a refreshing drink. Water in its solid phase is ice, and water in its gas phase is steam.

A simple way to describe a substance is by its phase at room temperature, which is approximately 73.4 degrees Fahrenheit (23 degrees Celsius). Water's phase at room temperature is liquid. Silver, like all the metals except mercury, is a solid at room temperature.

The Color Silver

It might seem obvious, but one notable property of silver is its color. Silver has a shiny gray-white appearance. It might even be said that silver has a silver color! This is in contrast to the color of some other metals—such as reddish copper and yellowish gold. When polished, silver reflects light better than any other metal. Because of this property, silver is used to make high-quality mirrors.

Shaping Silver

Malleability is the capability of silver to be bent, shaped, and pounded into sheets. Silver is one of the most malleable of all the metals. This property enables a piece of silver to be beaten into a thin sheet

Silver sheets can be rolled thin enough that artisans can hammer designs into them.

Silver as a Catalyst

A catalyst is a substance that increases the rate of a chemical reaction. The catalyst itself does not undergo any chemical change. Silver's chemical properties make it an ideal catalyst, especially in the production of two highly used industrial chemicals: ethylene oxide and formaldehyde. Ethylene oxide is a basic component for items molded of plastic and is also used to make antifreeze coolant for cars. Formaldehyde helps make solid plastics and is used in everything from plywood to electronic equipment.

0.0025 inches (0.0635 millimeters) thick known as leaves. Silver's malleability is also the reason it can be shaped into intricate pieces of jewelry and silverware.

Ductility is the ability to be stretched into wires. Silver is very ductile. Less than half an ounce of the metal can be stretched into a wire more than 1 mile (1.6 kilometers) long. Metals that are ductile are often used to make electrical wire. Copper is most commonly used for this purpose because it is inexpensive.

How Hard Is Silver?

Silver is a relatively soft metal so it is often combined with other metals to harden it. These mixtures of metals are known as alloys. A well-known silver alloy is sterling silver, which is 92.5 percent silver and 7.5 percent copper. The addition of copper makes the metal less likely to bend or become misshapen. This is important in the manufacture of products like silverware. A pure silver knife or fork would be too soft to use as an eating utensil.

Scientists measure hardness using the Mohs scale. The scale ranges from one to ten, with one representing the softest substance (talc) and ten representing the hardest (diamond). Silver has a value of 2.5 on the Mohs scale, which makes it slightly harder than gold but softer than most other metals.

Conducting Electricity and Heat

Electricity is the flow of electrons through a substance. Silver conducts electricity because

Silver is a better conductor of electricity than any other element. As such, it is often used in cables.

its sole outer-shell electron can easily move from atom to atom. When voltage is applied, the electrons are set in motion, creating an electrical current. Silver is a better conductor of electricity than any other element, which makes it valuable in electronics and electrical industries.

In nearly the same way that silver conducts electricity, it also conducts heat. When stirring a cup of hot cocoa with a pure silver spoon, the spoon handle becomes hot much more quickly than with a steel or plastic spoon. Like its ability to conduct electricity, silver is better than all the other elements at conducting heat.

Silver's Melting and Boiling Points

The melting point is the temperature at which a substance changes from solid to liquid. Silver's melting point is 1,763°F (962°C). That is much hotter than the average home oven. This property also makes silver a valuable element. Silver can be used at high temperatures and still retain its strength and structural integrity.

The boiling point is the temperature at which a substance changes from liquid to gas. Silver has a very high boiling point of 4,014°F (2,212°C).

Mass Per Volume

Density is the measure of mass per volume. It is usually measured in grams per cubic centimeter (g/cm^3). Something that is dense is compact, meaning a lot of mass is packed into a small space.

Silver has a density of 10.5 g/cm^3. Compare that to the density of aluminum at 2.7 g/cm^3. Silver is almost four times as dense as aluminum. Compare a piece of aluminum and a piece of silver of the same size. The piece of silver would be almost four times as heavy.

Silver may seem dense compared to aluminum, but compared to gold it is not dense at all. In fact, gold (19.3 g/cm^3) is nearly twice as dense as silver.

3

Finding Silver

‖‖

Silver is found in the rocks of Earth's crust, known as ores. An example of a silver ore is argentite, which consists of silver combined with the element sulfur in a ratio of two atoms of silver to one atom of sulfur.

Silver ores are not easy to find. Geologists estimate that for every 1 billion pounds (454 million kilograms) of rock on Earth there are only 70 pounds (32 kg) of silver.

Sometimes the metal is concentrated in deposits known as lodes or veins, which have been a popular source of silver for thousands of years. The Comstock Lode was a famous lode discovered in Nevada in 1859. It yielded hundreds of millions of dollars' worth of silver over a twenty-year period. By 1880, most of the lode's silver had been removed, so mining it was no longer profitable.

Silver ore is found in the rocks of Earth's crust.

The Discovery of Silver

The first silver mines were discovered in Greece and modern-day Turkey nearly 5,000 years ago. Silver from these mines was worked into jewelry, bowls, cups, and other objects by skilled craftspeople. Because silver was desired by many ancient cultures, the groups or nations that controlled the sources of silver often became very wealthy and powerful.

About 600 BCE, large silver deposits were discovered near Athens, Greece. Known as the mines of Laurion, their silver helped build the Greek empire. The Roman people also used silver to finance their empire. Most of their silver came from mines in Spain, over which they had gained control after winning the Second Punic War in 202 BCE. With a ready source of silver, both the Greeks and the Romans began using silver coins. The ancient Greeks traded the drachma, while the Romans minted a coin called the denarius. These coins ranged in weight from one-eighth to one-seventh of an ounce (or three and a half to four grams).

The Spanish mines controlled by the Romans were an important source of silver for nearly one thousand years. More large mines were discovered in Germany and Eastern Europe during medieval times (CE 800–1200). The silver from these mines was traded all over Europe, Asia, and North Africa. In China, silver was often exchanged for the exotic spices and silk craved by Europeans.

New World Silver

In 1492, Christopher Columbus (1451–1506) landed in the Caribbean and claimed land for the king of Spain. He was soon followed by Spanish soldiers and explorers known as conquistadors. These men were driven by the desire to find silver and gold.

One famous conquistador was Francisco Pizarro (circa 1475–1541). His small army conquered the Incas, the native people of Peru, and claimed their vast stores of gold and silver. Pizarro's victory, however, cost him his life. In 1541, he was murdered by a rival group of Spanish soldiers who wanted a larger share of the Incan treasure.

The conquistadores discovered silver mines throughout Central and South America. One of the most profitable was the Potosí mine in Bolivia, which shipped millions of ounces of silver back to the king of Spain.

For the next three hundred years, mines in Bolivia, Peru, and Mexico produced the majority of the world's silver. In the mid-nineteenth century, the state of Nevada became a hot spot for silver. Rich deposits like the Comstock Lode drew hundreds of miners and prospecting companies seeking to strike it rich. Smaller

The Comstock Lode was the first major silver discovery in the United States. People flocked to California, Colorado, Nevada, and Utah in search of silver.

mines were discovered in Utah and Colorado. About this time, advances in technology made it less dangerous and easier to mine silver.

Mining for Silver

Silver mining is a global industry and operates in markets worldwide. The output of silver from mining is measured in metric tons. One metric ton is equal to 2,205 pounds or 1,000 kilograms. Since the sixteenth century, much of the world's silver has come from Central and South America. Mexico produces the most silver and is home to one of the most productive silver companies in the world. Peru has large reserves of the metal and is the second-largest silver producer.

The greatest demand for silver is by the jewelry industry. The next highest demand of the metal is for use in coins and silver bars, silverware, and in industrial fabrication for electronics and photography.

Top Silver-Producing Countries

	Metric tons/yr
1. Mexico	5,600
2. Peru	4,100
3. China	3,600
4. Chile	1,500
5. Australia	1,400
6. Poland	1,400
7. Russia	1,400
8. Bolivia	1,300
9. United States	1,100

Source: U.S. Geological Survey, 2017.

Flotation separation involves mixing ore, water, and chemicals until the ores separate and can be skimmed out.

Separating Silver from Metal Ores

Lodes, or veins, are metals sandwiched between layers of rock. For centuries, high concentrations of silver ores, such as the Comstock Lode, were a major source of silver. However, these sources have become harder to find. Today, silver is often the by-product of processing other metal ores, such as lead, zinc, and copper.

Galena is an example of lead ore that is mined for its lead content, but also produces small amounts of silver. In a mine, galena ore is drilled and blasted from the surrounding rock. The ore is then ground into powder by rock-crushing equipment.

The next step is known as flotation separation The ore, water, and special chemicals are mixed in a container. This mixture is agitated to create air bubbles. Metals in the mixture attach to the air bubbles and rise to the top. The metals are then skimmed out of the container. The collection of finely powdered metals is partially melted to remove sulfur and oxygen impurities. It is then completely melted in a furnace in a process known as smelting. This process removes additional impurities, such as the element antimony. The molten mixture is poured into a container of pure, molten lead that is hot at the top and cooler at the bottom. As the molten mixture is added to the container, the silver turns into crystals and floats to the surface because silver has a higher melting point than lead. This allows silver to be separated from the lead, which remains molten.

4

Ionic Bonds and Silver

A toms of different elements join together to form compounds. For example, silver and iodine atoms combine to form a compound called silver iodide.

The reason that atoms join with other atoms has to do with the valence, or outer-shell electrons. Chemical bonds result when atoms share or transfer valence electrons. Take silver iodide for example. Silver has one electron in its outer shell, while iodine has seven. Atoms with a filled outer shell of electrons are more stable.

When an atom of iodine comes near a silver atom, it pulls away silver's lone outer electron. By gaining one electron, an iodine atom gets a filled outer shell and becomes more stable. As a result, iodine gains an electron and becomes a negative ion. By losing an electron and forming a cation, the silver atom also achieves a filled outer electron shell and becomes more stable. Silver loses an electron and becomes a positive ion.

These oppositely charged ions are attracted to each other and form a chemical bond known as an ionic bond. Compounds that form ionic bonds are known as ionic compounds.

Equations and Reactions

Chemical formulas are a shorthand way of describing compounds. The chemical formula indicates which atoms are bound together and in

Silver and iodine atoms combine to form a compound called silver iodide.

what ratio. For example, the formula for silver iodide is AgI. Ag is the chemical symbol for silver, while I is the chemical symbol for iodine. The elements combine in an atomic ratio of one to one. In other words, one atom of silver combines with one atom of iodine.

Ag_2S is the chemical formula for a compound called silver sulfide. The "2" to the right of the symbol for silver indicates that there

Creating Alloys

Mixtures of two or more metals are called alloys. An alloy is not a compound because the elements in the mixture do not combine in fixed ratios. In the compound silver iodide, silver and iodine atoms always combine in a ratio of two to one. However, in an alloy, the atoms of the different metals can combine in nearly any ratio. It is like mixing together different colors of paint, or mixing together nuts, raisins, and pretzels to make a snack mix. Silver forms alloys with a number of different metals. One alloy of silver has its own name, electrum. Electrum is a pale yellow alloy of silver and gold that occurs naturally and has been valued since ancient times.

are two atoms of silver (and one atom of sulfur) in each molecule of silver sulfide.

Chemical reactions are described by chemical equations. The reaction between silver and iodine forms silver iodide. Iodine is represented as I_2 because it has two atoms in a molecule, and silver is represented as Ag because it is not molecular. The chemical equation for this reaction is:

$$2 \text{ Ag (s)} + I_2 \text{ (g)} \rightarrow 2\text{AgI (s)}$$

In all chemical equations, the substance or substances to the left of the arrow are known as the reactants. The substance or substances to the right of the arrow are called the product. The equation shows that two atoms of silver combine with two atoms of iodine to form silver iodide. The "s" indicates that the silver and silver iodide are solids. The "g" indicates that the iodine is a gas. (At room temperature, iodine is a solid.)

Silver halides are ionic compounds made of silver and a halogen. All ionic compounds of silver are sensitive when exposed to light. They were used to make photographic and X-ray film before digital imaging systems were invented.

Compounds of Silver and a Halogen

Silver halides are ionic compounds made of silver and a halogen. (A halogen is any of the elements from group VIIA of the periodic table.) The three most important silver halides are silver bromide (AgBr), silver chloride (AgCl), and silver iodide (AgI).

All ionic compounds of silver are, to some degree, sensitive when exposed to light. All three of these silver compounds were used to make photographic and X-ray film before the development of digital systems. When light struck the film, it caused the silver halide to break apart into silver atoms and halogen atoms. The silver atoms, which were darker than the silver halide compound, deposited on the film. The film was then developed to bring out the image.

The process of developing a silver exposure involved a chemical reaction in which silver halide was converted to silver metal. This reaction was speeded up by the tiny particles of silver formed when the film was exposed. Therefore, the developed image was darkest where the silver halide was exposed and turned into silver particles. In essence, a photograph or X-ray was an image drawn with silver.

Silver iodide is also used to artificially produce rain. This procedure, known as cloud seeding, has been used in areas that are experiencing severe drought. In cloud seeding, airplanes are used to spray silver iodide into a cloud. The silver iodide causes water droplets to form into ice crystals, which fall out of the cloud. As the ice crystals fall, they melt and turn into rain.

A Poisonous Compound

Silver nitrate ($AgNO_3$) is a colorless compound that is made by reacting silver with nitric acid (HNO_3). It is poisonous and must be handled carefully, being commonly used in the preparation of silver halides for photographic film.

The equation below shows how silver nitrate reacts with table salt (NaCl) to create silver chloride. The "aq" in parentheses stands for "aqueous," which means that the compounds are dissolved in water.

$$AgNO_3 \text{ (aq)} + NaCl \text{ (aq)} \rightarrow AgCl \text{ (s)} + NaNO_3 \text{ (aq)}$$

The reaction results in solid silver chloride gathering on the bottom of the container in which the reactants are mixed. The formation of a solid when two liquids are mixed is known as a precipitation reaction.

In the past, eye drops of 1 percent silver nitrate solution were used to prevent eye infections in newborns. This is because silver nitrate kills bacteria. Today, antibiotics are more commonly used for this purpose.

Why Silver Tarnishes

When an object made of silver is exposed to air long enough, it loses its shine and turns dull gray or black. This is known as tarnishing. Silver objects tarnish because they react with hydrogen sulfide (H_2S) in the air to create a thin layer of silver sulfide (Ag_2S).

Some foods, such as mustard and eggs, contain sulfur and can tarnish silver objects. If a silver knife is used to put mustard on a sandwich, it has to be washed off quickly. Otherwise, the knife might become coated with silver sulfide.

When an object made of silver is exposed to air long enough, it loses its shine and turns dull gray or black. This is known as tarnishing.

Argentite is silver sulfide that occurs naturally in Earth's crust. It is also known as acanthite. The Comstock Lode in Nevada was a famous deposit of argentite that was mined for its silver content.

More Silver Compounds

Besides silver halides, silver also forms numerous other compounds. Many of these have important uses in medicine and industry. For example, silver sulfadiazine ($C_{10}H_9AgN_4O_2S$) is used to treat burns, silver fulminate (AgCNO) is a powerful explosive used to make fireworks, and silver oxide (Ag_2O) is used to make batteries. Like the silver halides, these compounds are ionic—they consist of positively charged silver ions combined with negatively charged ions.

5

Silver in Daily Life

//

Silver's chemical and physical properties make it a useful element. For example, since polished silver reflects light better than any other metal, silver is used to make high-quality mirrors. Silver halides are critical in the manufacture of photographic film. Of course, silver is used for much more than making mirrors and film. Silver is almost everywhere in your everyday life.

Uses of Silver at Home

Of all the elements, silver is the best conductor of electricity. It is such a good conductor that very little silver is needed to pass an electrical current.

Beneath every key in a computer keyboard are two thin patches of silver separated by a tiny space, which is called a silver membrane switch.

Beneath every key in a computer keyboard are two thin patches of silver separated by a tiny space, which is called a silver membrane switch. When a key is pressed, the two patches touch, sending an electrical current that races toward the computer's central processing unit. The end result is a letter appearing on the computer screen.

Silver is ideal for this task because it is extremely sensitive. It only takes a light touch of the key to produce the current. Silver is also durable. If the key is hit repeatedly the silver contact will not fail.

Measuring Silver's Purity

Fineness is the measure of the purity of silver. To determine fineness, multiply the percentage of silver in a sample by 10. Sterling silver, which is 92.5% silver, has a fineness of 925 (92.5 x 10). Less expensive silver often has a fineness near 800. The most pure type of silver is known as fine silver. It has a fineness of at least 999.

Silver membrane switches are used in many other machines. According to the Silver Institute, "Every time a homeowner turns on a microwave oven, dishwasher, clothes washer, or television set, the action activates a switch with silver contacts that completes the required electrical circuit."

Inside a computer is a circuit board made of thin plastic with small circular and rectangular pieces of metal stuck to it. The surface of the circuit board has a mazelike pattern of lines. These devices are also found in mobile phones, electrical appliances, and televisions. Circuit boards often use silver. A silver alloy, known as solder, is used as a glue to attach the components to the board and ensure that electricity flows freely.

Silver and Money

Silver was first used as a coin more than 2,500 years ago. Because silver is malleable, it can be shaped into a thin, round coin and is soft enough for a design to be stamped on it. This design might

The Walking Liberty half dollar was issued from 1916 to 1947. It was 90 percent silver and 10 percent copper.

identify the nation that issued the coin, but can also designate the coin's value.

Today all nations have removed their silver coins from circulation because silver has become too expensive. The silver content in a coin, if made today, would be worth more than the face value of the coin. The United States last issued silver coins in 1965. In England, silver coins were last minted in 1947. However, many countries still release commemorative silver coins to honor famous people, places, or events. These coins are popular with collectors, and most of them increase in value.

Pure silver is bought and sold on the international silver market. The major centers for trading silver are New York, Chicago, London, Zurich, Paris, Frankfurt, and Hong Kong. Silver is bid on and purchased, often by companies that use the metal to manufacture products. Individuals also buy silver as an investment. The market price of silver changes daily. In 2017 the average price of silver was between fifteen and twenty dollars an ounce (0.03 kg).

The Many Forms of Silver

Silver is the ideal metal for jewelry. It is soft enough to be shaped and stretched, yet durable enough to withstand regular wear and tear. It can also be polished to create a spectacular, reflective surface. Mixed with other metals to create alloys, silver's hardness and color can be customized to meet the needs of the artist.

Forks, knives, and spoons made out of sterling silver are valued for their beauty. However, since silver is not the most affordable metal, a lot of silverware today is made of less-expensive metal, like stainless steel. Silver-plated silverware is also popular.

In silver plating, an object made out of less expensive metal is coated, or plated, with a thin layer of silver. It is done by placing the object in a solution of silver cyanide, along with a bar of silver. The object to be plated and the bar of silver are connected to a battery.

Vases, serving platters, and silverware that are made out of sterling silver are valued for their beauty.

This causes the silver bar to dissolve, forming silver ions that replace those that were deposited on the object. The silver ions flow through the solution to deposit onto the object.

Silver was also once commonly used to fill cavities in teeth. The filling was a mixture, or amalgam, of silver, mercury, tin, copper, and zinc. The amalgam was a soft paste that, when applied to a tooth, quickly hardened and expanded to create a durable filling. Today, cavities are more commonly filled with composite resins that match the color of teeth.

Silver's Valuable Future

There is no doubt that silver has a bright future. It is used in cars, cell phones, and computers. It is also used on the International Space Station; in 2015, NASA approved a plan to use the Russian method of purifying water by using antibacterial silver. Ionized silver was shown to be easier and more effective and efficient at purifying water on the station. Back on Earth, the Food and Drug Administration) is less keen on using silver in this way, but wherever the future takes us, silver will probably be there in one form or another!

Glossary

atom The smallest unit of an element.

compound A substance made up of two or more elements bound together by chemical bonds.

conduct To allow something, such as heat or electricity, to pass through.

current The flow of electrically charged particles.

density The mass of a sample divided by its volume.

ductile Capable of being stretched into a wire.

electron A negatively charged particle found outside of the nucleus, or center, of an atom.

ion A positively or negatively charged atom or group of atoms.

matter Anything that has mass and exists as a solid, liquid, or gas.

molecule Two or more atoms joined together by chemical bonds.

neutron A particle without charge that is part of the nucleus of most atoms.

ore A rock that contains a valuable metal.

proton A positively charged particle that is part of the nucleus of an atom.

radioactive Capable of releasing high-energy rays or particles.

talc A very soft mineral also known as magnesium silicate.

valence electron An electron in the outer shell of an atom.

Further Reading

Dingle, Drian, and Dan Green. *The Complete Periodic Table: All the Elements with Style!* New York, NY: Kingfisher, 2015.

DK. *The Elements Book: A Visual Encyclopedia of the Periodic Table.* New York, NY: DK Children, 2017.

Gray, Theodore. *The Elements: A Visual Exploration of Every Known Atom in the Universe.* New York, NY: Black Dog & Leventhal, 2012.

Green, Dan. *Scholastic Discover More: The Elements.* New York, NY: Scholastic Reference, 2012.

Websites

Housing a Forest

housingaforest.com/silver-egg-experiment/
Make a silver-colored egg at home!

Silver Facts

sciencekids.co.nz/sciencefacts/metals/silver.html
Find out more about the silver atom and its properties.

Thought Co

thoughtco.com/interesting-silver-element-facts-603365
Read some fun facts about silver.

Bibliography

Atkins, P. W. *The Periodic Kingdom: A Journey into the Land of the Chemical Elements.* New York, NY: Basic Books, 1995.

Ball, Philip. *The Ingredients: A Guided Tour of the Elements.* Oxford, England: Oxford University Press, 2002.

Coffey, Rebecca. "20 Things You Didn't Know About the Periodic Table." *Discover Magazine*, November 20, 2011. http://discovermagzine.com/2011/nov/20-things-you-didn't-know-about-periodic-table.

Dartmouth Toxic Metals: Superfund Research Program. "The Facts on Silver." November 29, 2010. https://www.dartmouth.edu/~toxmetal/toxic-metals/more-metals/silver-faq.html.

Emsley, John. *Nature's Building Blocks: An A-Z Guide to the Elements.* Oxford, England: Oxford University Press, 2001.

Fazekas, Andrew. "Silver in Space: Metal Found to Form in Distinct Star Explosion." *National Geographic*, September 9, 2012. https://www.google.com/amp/s/relay.Nationalgeographic.com/proxy/distribution/public/amp/news/2012/09/120907-Silver-gold-star-explosions-su-pernovae-science-hansen.

Friend, J. Newton. *Man and the Chemical Elements.* New York, NY: Charles Scribner's Sons, 1961.

Geoscience Australia. "Silver Mineral Fact Sheet." Australian Atlas of Mineral Resources, Mines, and Processing Centres. 2003. Retrieved October 11, 2005. http://www.australianminesatlas.gov.au.

Lindsay, David. "The Wizard of Photography." 1999. Retrieved October 11, 2005. http://www.pbs.org/wgbh/amex/eastman/ index.html.

Lovett, Chip, and Raymond Chang. *Understanding Chemistry.* New York, NY: McGraw-Hill, 2005.

Nogrady, Bianca. "Your Old Phone Is Full of Untapped Precious Metals." BBC News, October 18, 2016. http:www.bbc.com/future/story/20161017-your-old-phone-is-full-of-precious-metals.

Royal Society of Chemistry. "Periodic Table: Silver," Periodic Table, 2017. http://www.rsc.org/periodic-table/element/47/silver.

Show Me Science: Chemistry: Periodic Table of Elements. TMW Media Group, 2012.

Silver Institute. "The Indispensable Metal." Retrieved October 11, 2005. http://www.silverinstitute.org.

Space News, "NASA Open to Using Silver-Treated Water in Space Despite FDA Opposition." Retrieved October 2017. http://www.space.news/2016-06-06-nasa-open-to-using-silver-treated-water-in-space-despite-fda-opposition.html.

Zumdahl, Steven S. *Chemistry.* Lexington, MA: D. C. Heath and Company, 1989.

Index